THE
SOBER
POET

A Collection Of Poems From A
Recovered Alcoholic

Liza Roe

THE SOBER POET

Cover illustration and interior illustrations by Ali Cushing

liza.roe.outspoken

An inspiring and emotive collection of poetry
about one alcoholic's experience,
strength and hope in recovery.

Table of Contents

Circumstantial Happiness	7
A Grateful Alcoholic	10
Pick Your Poison	11
Worst Day Sober	12
Lacking Love	14
Don't Wait	15
Relapse	16
One Day at a Time	17
No Smoking	19
Never Again	20
Reckless Driving	21
That's It, I Quit	22
Recovery of Sanity	23
Trustworthy	25
A Way Out	26
I Will Survive	28
The Dangers of Complacency	30
Just Take the Stairs	31
Let Go and Let God	32
Committed	33
Learning to Swim	34
The Key is Willingness	36
Coming Back to Love	38
Forest Fires	40
Pause When Agitated	42
Hollow Bones	43
Moral Inventory	45

Break Down	46
Relief at Last	47
Mirror Marvels	48
Only as Sick as Our Secrets	49
The Seed	51
Flooded with Feeling	52
Awareness in Action	54
Overdue Amends	56
It's Never Too Late	58
Hidden Talents	59
Things I've Gained	60
Acceptance of All Selves	61
Moment to Moment	63
High on Life	64
Forgetting Expectations	66
Not a Normal Drinker	67
I Woke Up Like This	68
Unicorn	70
Hole in the Soul	72
My Old Way of Thinking	73
Coffee Cancellation	74
Who I Used to Be	76
Two Wolves	78
No Longer a Liar	80
Old Acquaintances and New Conceptions	81
Rocky Bottoms	83
A Moment of Silence	84
Spark of Hope	85
Primary Purpose	87
Carry Your Message	88

Circumstantial Happiness

Every morning after, I experienced an identity crisis
Because I didn't know what I did and who I was last night...
What messes I made...
All I knew was it's SaturDAY morning
And it's time to DAY drink
But I was still hungover from the night before last
Because I suffered from circumstantial happiness.
If you did this and didn't do that, I'll be happy.
Just do what I tell you and listen to what I say.
Obey every word so that I can know
What to expect from the world
Because unpredictability is scary.

Let me offer my assistance,
Share advice that's unsolicited.
I didn't know that helpfulness was the sunny side of control
Until I realized that I was *too* helpful
And people wouldn't listen.
My resentments would swelter in the sun,
I felt alone and I knew that no one would understand...
I was on a one-woman mission to figure out how to live.

But I became suspicious when the drink no longer delayed
My fictitious reality.
Not only was I afraid of what would happen
And where I would end up,
I was terrified of who I would become.
But really, I never knew who I was...
Even in sobriety, it took time to gain clarity
Around the simple question of...
"Who am I?"

Now I know that I am me.
I have a fluid sense of identity.
I am not defined by any one thing.

I don't become tied to any thought or idea,
I let my life shift naturally.
I use my intuition to handle situations which once were baffling
And I have a strong sense of oneness, of unity.

I have people who care about my whereabouts;
They listen when I share about life
And the struggles I experience.
When I can't see something with my own two eyes,
They bring in new awareness.
They tell me it's okay to not be okay,
That I don't need to grin and bear it any longer.
So now I honor each emotion,
Knowing all the while that embracing each ocean of feeling
Simply makes me stronger and a more authentic human being.

They remind me not to judge any person,
To practice love and tolerance
When I'm faced with an inner adverse reaction
And now I can respond
Because I am honest,
Open-minded and willing to let go,
Not hold on.
To trust that a higher power has my back
Even when my eyes are closed.
I know I will be given the serenity to detach
From that which attracts
My inner calamity and chaos.

Today I have choices...
I can choose to feel lost
Or change my perspective,
Live in the present
And be grateful for what's to come,
Equally so for where I was.
My gratitude is not able to be measured,
It is indefinite.
Living life this way has been an absolute pleasure.
Now, if you want what I have

It's right here,
All you need to do is come get it.

A Grateful Alcoholic

Hi, my name is Liza
I am a grateful alcoholic
That's right, I said "grateful"
Call it what you wanna
A curse
A shameful display of all my traits
Bathed in fire
Burned to ash
Then raised from the dead
Now my shame resides in the past

Fake it 'til you make it so I act "as if"
I'm being guided by God
We've had some unpleasant tiffs
Back when I was closed off
But now I'm baptized by sin
Catapulted into the fourth dimension
Foundation built on new perspective
Ten, no, twelve steps ahead

I'm grateful for that time my chin ate the curb
I lost two teeth and damaged the nerves

I'm grateful for that time my car rolled down a hill
While I was stealing flowers from someone else's field

I'm grateful for that time I was pulled over and arrested
On account of being stubborn and failing a field sobriety test

I'm grateful for that time I was escorted out of the bar
And then recklessly agreed to get into a strange man's car

I'm grateful to be alive when there is no reason I should be
So yes, that's right, I'm a grateful alcoholic
And I am blessed by tragedy

Pick Your Poison

"Pick your poison," he said
As if I had a choice to listen

Gripping the table
Just one slip up
And I'll be able
To feel okay again

Peeling back the layers of my skin
Dealing with the hand I was given
Feeling a resistance
Praying to something I'm not familiar with
But only in
Times of trouble
So I talk but never listen

Fiending for that good shit
My need to be numbed
Is stronger than my lack of love
So pump me up
With all the drugs
And alcohol
Cause that's the only way
I feel at all

So I'll pick my poison
Because I have no choice when
My ego is completely in control

Worst Day Sober

"The worst day sober is better than the best day drunk."

Well, fuck
I call bullshit
You must not have drank
The way I did

It was a nonstop party
Pity uninvited
Remind me why
I stopped drinking again?
Oh yeah, that's right
Cause I was just pretending
To play a part

Learning how to let loose
And lose control of the noose
I had customized for the purpose
Of identity abuse

Duality infused
Confused on which me to choose
I grew up not knowing who I was
I thought liquor was helping me grow the fuck up
But it wasn't

I let an inebriated inner child
Take the wheel
Driving us both
To an unrecognizable hell

Broken spells and empty bottles
Eventually ran out of lies to swallow
Rationalization not probable

Relying on a higher power,
Not-God

Ever-present, sometimes unheard
If I'm not listening
Or if I'm writing words

My worst days sober
Are really not too bad
When I consider
The drunk memories I had

I can't change the past
But the sober version of myself
Sees all the blessings I have
She counts them daily,
She's grateful for those acts

The best days now
Are the ones without
Drugs and alcohol
Because now I remember
The person I once was

Lacking Love

The crushing weight of indignation
Provokes me to an almost catatonic state

Pour another vodka tonic just to stay awake
She can't eat
Sleep escapes
But I breathe freely in the wake of her absence
Tragic, I know

I show no emotion
Grow colder with each shoulder turned
A deficit of dopamine has me cured
Of all feeling
And I become lost in catacombs frosted over
My glossy ledger reads
"Here lies her sanity"

Don't Wait

Today's the day
I won't drink
But today is tomorrow
So maybe I'll wait
Because tomorrow isn't today

I could save myself some trouble
If I just halted the struggle
Yesterday

But instead I'll wait
Carry the shame
Because my sick brain
Thinks it makes me stronger
Can't concede that I need to alter
My state of being

In a place of dire unmanageability...

I will die
If I don't change
The way I'm living

Relapse

I am an alcoholic,
I'm no longer a psycho
But if you tap into my crazy
A few fuses might blow

Breathalyzer burden disposed of
Far from Tuesdays that are too turned up
Never again is not soon enough

Then I relinquish a closed mouth laugh
Jaw unhinged
Blood lust rushes to my head
I am prepared to sin again

My thirst needs to be quenched
So I start swallowing water
Straight from my devil's hands

One Day at a Time

I had a rabid dislike of false experts
DIY mindset
An independence curse
I'll do it myself especially when it hurts
I can figure it out
Let me try this first
Then it's gets worse

I can't solve the problem
Staring at the mirror
Screaming
"What is wrong with me?!"

Punitive procrastination
Why am I waiting?
Later, later, later
Distractions follow my heaving hollowed spurts of effort
Coquettish indulgence in cybersex work

Careless annulment of self-love
Curt words spur negativity
I hear echoes of my past self whisper
"Do it later"
They sing to me
"Later, later, later"

Then it's too late
Step backwards towards relapse
Instincts on a rampage balk at investigation
I sleuth for clues to my soul's segregation
Separated from self
Trepidation quells
In my gut
Trigger finger lingers
But it's stuck

Back to basics
I've had enough of poor me, poor me
Pity party for three
Pour me a glass of holy water
I am parched but never far from a source

So I choose to rejoice
For the life that I have
Cradled by connection and unity
I was carried to a hidden path
Saved from self-destruction
Ask me if I want another option
And I can barely stop myself from saying
Maybe later, just not today

No Smoking

Endorphins are the devil
But I'm feeling disconnected and desperate

Don't know why I let it get to me

I know that smoke won't settle
Those feelings of isolation

Be patient child
I remind myself
While I'm waiting

Focus more so on consciously creating
And those feelings will dissipate

Give it time
Make a rhyme
Sing yourself a song
You'll be fine

Never Again

I *will* never drink again
Surrender from within
Beginning to begin
A new way of living

Romanticizing alcohol
Smashing illusions of control

Sobriety is for warriors
Who walk through life
Internalizing character

No more managing moods
Restrictive ideas grew
Then shrunk
No longer stuck

Become a survivor
Impending okay over chaos
Accepting defeat
Over the payoff
Of denial and drinking

Eternal longing for spiritual connection
Tranquility terminates my mental obsession

Then comes the question...
Will I drink again?

Because feelings don't go away
Taking things one day at a time
I swear surrender to win
I will *never* drink again

Reckless Driving

My alcoholic self
Was driving me to hell
For awhile

I asked, then demanded she slow down,
"You made a wrong turn"
"Have you learned nothing over the years?!"
"Put this car in reverse right now, young lady!"
Too late

She's duct taped my mouth
And stuffed me in the trunk

I tell her,
"Good luck trying to parallel park!"
She doesn't give a fuck
She think she drives better
When she's stoned and it's dark
Fucking idiot
Can she not see how addicted she is?
That the urge to resist no longer exists?

She's a slave to nothing but trouble
Eventually I hit that bitch with a shovel
She's lucky she's not dead
Now I'm driving this bus
And it's full speed ahead

That's It, I Quit

Weed,
Marijuana,
Cannabis,
I kinda wanna hit of it

But I quit,
I'm done with it,
If I do it again
I'll be full of regret
Cause I already decided
I'm done getting high

But I swear I need a vice sometimes,
Life is hard when I try to start
New habits all of a sudden,
It takes small steps
It doesn't
Happen overnight

Really though, it did this time,
I'm choosing now to find
Other ways of coping
So here's hoping
That this sticks
Cause that's it,
I quit,
I'm moving on

Recovery of Sanity

It's gonna be fun
Because I'm drunk
But it was never enough
To be so fucked up

A weekend warrior
Should've had many more DUIs
Because I drove drunk
So many times

I empathize with suicide
Bury me in the ground
In the hole I've dug out

Inner pain became
Greater than
The fear of change

I gave up
I surrendered
No longer a pretender
The power of prayer
Made this my last bender
Jails, institutions or death
To die like that
Is to die without dignity

My right to drink
Was soured by insane thinking
Hell on earth
Got worse and worse

Cup of noodles in my head
I'm on my way to wet brain
Or else I'll end up dead

Enter boredom
Read a book
Peace restored
Desire left
Reflect back...
The only limits that exist
Are the ones I create
When I resist

Living my way to a new way of thinking
One that isn't obsessive about drinking

Application of sacred selfishness
Praying for acceptance
And the release of expectations

The greatest thing I've come to know
Is that I know nothing
But that I want to stay sober

By the grace of God
On the path to wellness
Illness fading
First time I've felt this

God, grant me serenity
I will recover my belief
And be returned to sanity

Trustworthy

To trust or not to trust?
I lusted after a faith
I could not attain,
Reaching depths
Of exquisite pain,
Driving my own bus
And going the wrong way,
Don't overthink,
Do basic things daily,
Taking suggestions but suffering
From an impending sense of doom

Faith and fear can't exist
In the same space
Because faith is the fear
And trust is the action,
Fake it 'til you make it
Because I trust my own thinking,
I believed in God
But didn't trust it fully

My higher power knows what's best,
I can attest
That trusting HP
Has resulted in
More trust in me

A Way Out

A way out of depression
I continue to let it guide me
Shining light inside me
And across my shadow
Sweeping it away
But it's only in hiding

Waiting for a moment
To be accepted
And so I expect it
To writhe around in pain and regret
But I can change that
I can welcome it in
Hold it close and comfort it
It's within my power
To forgive all sin
I'm only human
I just needed to remind myself of this

So I am not disconcerted by setbacks
I trust the path ahead
From head to heart
I will turn my two halves
Into a whole
Embracing oneness
My authenticity unfolds

Integration of head and heart
Black and white
No more all or nothing mindset
This journey promises
Spiritual enlargement

I Will Survive

I am the victim
Of another addiction
I have multiple afflictions
That I must attend to consistently

Initially resistant to change
I loosened the reigns
And embraced a higher power
So that they could help me take life
Hour by hour
Day by day
Twenty-four hours at a time

As long as I am open to receiving
I am never denied love, caring
And a sense of belonging

Without my Higher P,
My life would have no meaning
I hold tight to the idea
That I am being divinely guided
That the inner strength
I hold inside me
Is inspired by my higher power

My highest self
Knows parts of my whole
Are quite unwell

Hour by hour
Day by day
I strain to remove
The toxicity
That has tried to change me

I remain
Through pain and struggle
Creatively shaping
A life I can love
I will not give up
I am a survivor
Of my addictions

The Dangers of Complacency

I've fallen off the path
Just slightly
Just enough to wanna slip
Myself back
Cause I see my mind wandering off
Thinking she's about to frolic
Through fields of clovers
But she's just stepping on
All those lucky little souls
Crushing their potential
And I'm over it

Time to start again
Slow and steady
With a handful of empathy
Cause she's clearly struggling
So I'll just be gentle
Tell her what's true
"I am brave"
"I am humble"
"And I'm grateful too"
I'll hold her hand
And guide her through
Because "I am strong"
And the life I choose
Is up to me

I believe that if I continue
On a spiritual path
I will be gifted all the answers
To the questions I asked
Self-doubt will subside
And clarity will find
It's way into my heart
And into my diseased mind

Just Take the Stairs

Scaling walls
In order to crawl
Out of the hole
I dug out

Put down the shovel
Trying to pull yourself up
Grabbing jagged rocks
Determined to prove
I don't need anyone's help

But I made it harder
Than it needed to be
Hanging for dear life
Incline increasing
Blisters on my fingers
And I'm tired of reaching

But I've come so far
Afraid to look down
I don't want to fall
Suddenly it's dawn
I rise with the sun

I look to my left
Strength renewed
And notice that this whole time
There's been a stairway to the view

Let Go and Let God

There is strength in surrender
God-willing, I am rendered complete
Acceptance of defeat
Cause I can barely control my own two feet
Let alone the spirits that be
They are guiding me divinely
As I seek inside me
For answers to questions
I've been trying to conceive

For too long, it feels like
I've been dying to breathe
Crying to release
Mines of dis-ease
My mind is diseased

Filing a cease and desist
Increase in commitment
Because my highest power
Knows no bounds
I am now committed
To my fucking self

Committed

Commitment -
The decision to submit oneself
To something else

Whether it's sobriety
Or someone you see exclusively

I've had trouble with it personally

But lately
I'm beginning to see
It's not as scary as I made it out to be

Taking things
One day at a time
Takes the pressure off
And I'm starting to find
Comfort in knowing
That things will work out
Exactly how they're supposed to

Learning to Swim

Slipping into sadness
I thought my brain was past this
Tragic carousel of madness

But I can't get away
I can't escape this plague
This sickness is cyclical
And it fills me with rage

Anger rooted in judgment of self
Polluting with drugs doesn't help anymore
Diluting with love lifts me up off the floor

Try as I might, as I must
I repair my concussed soul
Bereaved bondage of self
I break free from the hold
Admit my mind is unwell
I leap from this carousel
And I fall

I fell into a lake, a river, an ocean
Now I ache to deliver
The seed of a notion
That self-talk is made up
Our emotions are chosen
We can decide when's enough
Defrost what was frozen
Choose to give love to ourselves
First and foremost

The closer I get
To staying afloat
The less I regret
The pain I exposed

To myself and to others
Because I know now
That sooner or later
I'll be walking on water

The Key is Willingness

A temptress, a thief
Opted for picking locks
With no keys
Willing to kill myself
Self-will to the Nth degree
An extremist shamelessly drawn
To turning knobs
That didn't belong to me

Custodian role
Forced custody of
A jangling mangle of
Unidentifiable keys

I opened doors
To holes in walls
Uncovered unrest
Then recovered my cause

Carried the keys of willingness
Born found, then lost in a stillness
So uncomfortable
I added a shank
Making my keychain a killer

Locked out of the house
I was without
The key to my home
Because the mold
Was something I woefully buried
Thinking I was passed
The point of saving
But I wasn't

Trudged through the mud

With a suitcase of stuff
Eventually left it
And used the jagged edge
Of a rusty key
To jut open my door
And just like that
I was willing to do more

Coming Back to Love

Keep coming back,
Promises made will happen,
Seeking peace and understanding
To fill the emptiness inside me

My way wasn't working,
Consequences became
The cost of doing business
And I was tired of hurting

Finally put it together,
That every time there was an issue
I was either drinking or using

Keep coming back,
As I was destined to begin
A new way of life,
I started taking suggestions

My life was a nightmare,
Unmanageability had me scared,
Luxury became necessity,
I had a truly progressive allergy

Now my life is on the upswing,
No longer dodging responsibilities,
No longer smashing into trees,
Finding safety in sobriety

Practicing powerlessness,
Letting go of resistance,
Half measures availed me nothing,
Turning my life over to something else

Something greater,

Something I couldn't fathom,
I finally found where all the love I lost
Had gathered

Once the bottom was reached,
The lifestyle I was living
Came to a screeching halt

Recovery became a blessing,
Every day I am tested
In my belief in a higher power,
But I am capable of anything
With the new love I have found

Forest Fires

The forest and the trees...
I must separate them
To appease the chaos I cause

It's often my own fault
When I become lost
Amongst the trees

But all I need
Is another person to guide me

When they are suggesting
I am open minded
To accepting assistance
In extinguishing embers
Which were potentially risks
That might've stolen my surrender

Pause When Agitated

I don't drink because I'm an alcoholic
I don't smoke weed because I'm an alcoholic
I don't do hard drugs because I'm an alcoholic
Because anything I touch becomes a tonic
To wash down a false reality

But what I truly crave
What I really need
Is an influx of empathy
An upsurge in honesty
Divergence from grandiosity

I've seen proverbial prints
that incite profanity,
What the fuck do people want from me?
I can only take so much
Until I snap back from spirituality

Hollow Bones

Hollow bones hollowed out
To make way for soul growth
Token of appreciation
Low key I'm impatient but waiting
For the right time
For divinity to strike
To appear in my life
And steer me in the right direction
You have my attention

Tell me what to do
Suggest new tools
Because I have no clue
What I'm fucking doing
And I am of no use
When I am confused

Show me right from wrong
Turn tables on
My ego
We go
Into this
To trade ignorance
For bliss

Persist for the remedy
Persistency is key
And I am resilient
Steadfast I filter
I listen, I learn
Now it's my turn
To share happy, joyous and free

No fear, no envy
My insides are clean

My imagination, my dreams
Stagnation released

My will is not my own
It belongs to something greater
When I have hollow bones

Moral Inventory

Victimized by erratic emotions
Realizing they cause me chaotic commotion
Drop the word "blame" from my diction and vocab
I used to set conditions for despair in high doses
Expecting what isn't was my method of coping
But that line of thinking left me seemingly hopeless

Gifted self-awareness, my mind became open
"If you spot it, you got it"
A parable I heard in a particular program
No more excuses; revisit what I wrote up
Acceptance of my part
Admitting defects through disclosure

Accepting "what is" where others are concerned
If I live up to my potential,
I won't have step four to rework

Today, I accept "what is" instead of expecting "what isn't"
And this has left me seemingly hopeful for the present

Break Down

Break down
Now
Get there,
How?
Paralysis following
Analysis of self

Calling out to angels,
Make me able

No more fables and fiction,
I've made my decision

I am committed to self-care
And self-growth,
Gained awareness,
Now provoked
By my old
Paradigm

She pushed me off the cliff,
A new shift
But I choked
Cause I spoke too soon

Doomed to drown,
My indecisive ego
Burned down this house

Standing in the rubble
I struggle to rebuild
But I know that I will
Because I have been assigned
And this will only add
Fuel to my fire

Relief at Last

What does relief feel like?

I sit and I think
Stillness finds me
It takes time,
But once it comes
It is sweet and subtle
Organizing a gumbo pot
Of open-ended thoughts
Acceptance is key
Knowing that I control nothing
Except my mentality
And the reality I choose to believe
This is relief

My fears become apparent
Like a list of to-dos and pointless errands
They serve no use
Only paralyzing my time
And what I choose to do with it

Doubt and uncertainty
Stem from this fear
Condemning me to a spiral
But I don't want to be scared

I don't want to be afraid
I want to be fearless
So I decide to do it anyway
Freed from fear
I am released from dubiety
Relief is here
And I will not let it leave me

Mirror Marvels

As I speak
I can barely breathe
Meek-ish features
Surround my seat

As they speak
They look at me
Retracting me
From reverie

Officially an observer
Deservedly so
We all have the same right
To speak from our souls

As I look into their eyes
Something I had not expected
Their eyes glossy like mirrors
And I see myself reflected

Only as Sick as Our Secrets

Deluded disillusionment
Ego deflation
Humility got me through it when
I shared every horrible thing
I had ever done

Every shameful sin was lifted from
My shoulders
Halving problems
Rolling boulders
Whittled down by waterfalls
Of compassion and love

Instead of nurturing defects,
I broke the levy of my dammed-up emotions
Out of confinement
Conscious exposure

A flooding sense of relief
Overwhelmed by serenity
Only as sick as my secrets
Once I release them - emergence from isolation
Pain miraculously vanished
And I could finally stand
In stillness
Embracing a feeling of forgiveness
I had evaded
Because I felt undeserving
No doubt in my mind that living life alone is dangerous
Garbled rationalizations
And wishful thinking
Were well-intentioned
But halted healing
Sharing my faults with another promoted peace
And a new way of being

Now seeing I don't have to hold on to my wrongdoings
I can simply
let
them
go

The Seed

So many places to look
But all of it is in front of me
All that matters
All that I want to be

Proof of life had me hoping
I wouldn't be lonely any longer
And then I wasn't
I'm not stuck in comfortable chaos
I changed for the better
I was once lost
But then found
Sanity recovered
Mind sound

Spiritual solution dug up
From underground
The ringing in my ears
Gets loud and audible
When I hear angels
I know my soul is unstoppable
On this journey
Love becomes tangible

And I can finally see
All the way through the bottle
My spirit is freed
That seed that was planted
Becomes rooted
Somehow I managed
To sprout into a willow
A beautiful tree
That stands riverside
In soil that's clean

Flooded with Feeling

Damaged insides
Craving peace in the form of divine power
Show me how to live a life without struggle
Grasping at straws
My soul is in trouble

Coupled with self-hatred
Thrill-seeking and jaded
Created a life
With consequences horrific
Humiliation was common currency
And I had to pay it

The obsession wouldn't let me live without it
Confessing sins I thought would drown me

Treading water for decades
Conceding to myself
That I had lost my way

Surround me with love
So that I may stay above
These flooding feelings

Awareness in Action

Before I take action
I have to step back
Mentally
Just a bit
Then move through the moment mindfully
I can't have awareness
Unless I act accordingly
Swift action
Prevents me from
Acting passive
But what I want
Is to go slow
So I can consider
Passing thoughts
Instead of letting them take over
And attempt to run the whole show
A high level of mediocrity
Sheds light on where there's room to grow

And I let go
Let life guide me into
The action I was meant to own
Walk toward love and hold
My heart open
So I can receive that message of hope
Golden glow knows no limits
When I take action
I make a decision
To live my life
With humility
And other such characteristics

Submission to spirit
Grateful to hear that
If I move slowly

With kindness
I can easily be present
And this, to me
Is awareness in action

Overdue Amends

So many amends to be made
Delayed debts to be paid
Procrastinated by decades
And now my faith is shaking

I may have waited too long
To right these wrongs
My time to apologize
May have already come and gone

I may have to settle
For this rhyme of redemption
Too little too late
It is not my intention
To meddle in contention

If they've moved on
Then so can I
As my willingness is enough
To humble my pride

So I humbly admit
To the events I regret
If you don't want my apology
I'm okay with that

But if you would like to hear it
My only wish is to experience forgiveness
To accept accountability
For the stupid shit I did
Such as acting like
A selfish and inconsiderate bitch

Insecurities have left me
I can see the mistakes I've made clearly

So I hope you will forgive me
As I take ownership fearlessly

This year of calamity
Is my overdue release
Of lurking resentments and disservice
But I will not plead
I will simply state my apology
And that alone will set me free

It's Never Too Late

Fear and faith cannot coexist in the same space
But on the other side of fear is faith and freedom
Steeping for too long will leave tea bitter
And I'm a snob when it comes to good drinks

Trying to think, think, think my way out of fear
My dearest frenemy
If I take one drink, that drink takes a drink
Then the drink takes me

But it doesn't have to be that way anymore
I implore, I beg of my inner self
To be fearless and thorough from the very start
Try, I must or die, I will

Push past the fear
Because beyond that leering dread
Is an abundance of love
And an open heart full of acceptance
For all the parts I cannot change

I humbly ask someone to slap me on the hand
Just in case I ever forget
That my life is not a one-man-show
And I am most definitely not the host
I am just a portion of the whole

It gives me comfort to know
That almost everything is out of my control
I used to be scared so I couldn't let go absolutely
Until I truly understood that fear itself serves no good
Shoulda, woulda, coulda got this sooner
At least today, I can actually look in the mirror

Hidden Talents

I have many hidden talents,
Traits that challenge me
To become the person I want to be

Writing, singing...alcoholism

If you're observing my figure
You'd never know I had an affinity
For making poor decisions

Regrettable was my middle name,
Repetitive choices resulting in insane behavior,
Then I wrote it all down,
My soul became my savior,
Life was safer the more my soul took over,
Gave my old life the cold shoulder

Now I've integrated the past
To make myself whole
And I will never go back
To the way I was before

Hidden talents act as catalysts,
When I'm feeling stagnant
I simply catch a glimpse of what's hidden
And embrace it,
Enhance it without changing it,
Accept it for what it is

Writing, singing...alcoholism

Each one is a gift
Depending on how I look at it,
So these days I like to think
I'm actually pretty talented

Things I've Gained

The material gain
Is not worth the pain
I do it for the sake
Of divine change
Which is both intangible
And not able to be replaced

A purging of identity
Which was once wrapped up
In those material things
My only hope is sobriety
Restorative and free
It costs virtually nothing of me
Except a simple presence

There is no gain or greed
That is measurable by inches or feet
There is no thought
Of physical profit
The world stopped revolving
Around me

Spiritual sight recovered
So I was able to see
The "things" that I'm gaining everyday
Are just not things

Acceptance of All Selves

Self-destruction in the form of
Guilt-ridden, fear-driven
Pride and ego

It shows no remorse for the star role
And voiceover position,
An actor for the show
Who knows in their heart they are not deserving

Needing to examine moral inventory,
Fearful of true identity,
Emotional substance that cuts up
And inhibits my ability to see
With true perspective

No longer larger than life,
Becoming right-sized,
No longer a piece of shit
I was both selfish and inconsiderate

The stage character I used to present
Was identified in four steps

Progressive reputation,
Quarter-life crisis baited,
Then beaten,
Acknowledging judgement -
Resulting in freedom

Sincere effort relieved me
Of the double vision
I wasn't seeing

It was a double life I was leading,
She would sneak up on me, creeping

Initially drinking to ease my responsibilities
But she tried to take my whole life
And I sat by observing,
Afraid to speak up and state my purpose,
I felt worthless,
Skinless and shameful

Trying to hide painful
Past experiences
Instead of learning from them
But I'm done taking turns with that girl
Who was scared to live in a world
That didn't see her soul

Today, I constantly disclose
The thoughts I hold closest
And moment to moment
I find it gets easier
To accept the show
And go with the flow,
I'm not running things anymore
And neither is that girl

I am open
And have chosen
To embrace a new way,
Whole human experience,
Embodying mistakes
And a shameless aim
To accept all of myself
Regardless of what other people may say,
I love and accept
All of myself today

Moment to Moment

Being thankful in the moment
Grateful cause I know that
Anywhere I am is where I'm supposed to be

No doubt in my mind
That every life I live
Was saving me from sin
Lessons learned again and again
Hopeful doses doused get lit
By the fire started in my heart
Recoiled risk inspires a shift in thinking
Broken brain gone insane

Recovery of happiness
New perspective is a gift
Gratitude expressed daily
Twenty-four hours at a time
Led by divine powers
Not mine

And just like that
My life became finite
So I hold onto the light
Do the next right thing
And it all seems to work out
As long as I don't drink

High on Life

I'm so high on life that misery wants to tether me
Strap me to the ground
Slip me in a straitjacket and institutionalize my habit
Of snorting more than my fair share of joyful freedom

Crushing lines of life
Inhaling deeply through narrow holes
Into my empty and open soul

My body goes cold and numb with a pleasurable touch
Knowing that death is on my doorstep every moment
I'm sure that if I close my eyes,
I can relive that hopeful submissive event
When I gave up control and floated with my spirit

My dearest Ego,
It's time to take a vacation
Your services are no longer needed
Consider this your deflation

I've seen enough crazy to last an eternity
I've birthed a new phase
This is my millennium of maternity
Unearthed greener days
And now my life is flourishing
If the rain keeps a beat
Then a storm is a symphony
If I am complete
Then God is within me
If I can speak
Then I could share subliminally…

Or I could be
Direct with my words
Say what I actually mean

Quit fucking around with poetry
But if you've been listening
It's all the same thing
Isn't it?

Forgetting Expectations

Forget about the future
All is fundamentally well
Here and now
Simply stay sober
And everything will work out

Surface wrongness -
Don't let it upset us
I feel deeply secure
In the goodness and purpose
Occurring in the universe

The future takes care of itself
This day is all I have
A day in which
I may have a chance
To help somebody else

I am compelled
To expel all anxiety
Regarding the future
I am living presently
So that I can be of use
With a grateful heart

I've come to part
With expectations
I choose to live simply
And expect nothing in return

Not a Normal Drinker

Can I drink normally?
No

Can I stay sober?
Are you fucking kidding me?
You must be asking rhetorically
Cause the answer will forever be
Fuck yes, I can

I've proven
That I can persevere in
All that God's guidance
Moves me to do

I am led by the touch
Of a higher power
And divine principles

Today I know what is right and good
I've ceased fighting
With everything and everyone

God's guidance is often gradual
I know for a fact
That 1,000 drinks is never enough
And one is too many
That's what addiction was like
And I will not go back to that

I Woke Up Like This

I feel awake
Even if I got tired
I wouldn't go back to sleep
Not back to that dream
That shit was soul depleting
I really can't think of a single reason
I would get back in a bed
With those shitty ass sheets
I have no desire to repeat
Any action involving dirty laundry

Airing it out
Apparently now
Once awareness is found
I can't ignore it
Pouring bleach down the toilet
Because all that did to my bed was soil it

Royally fucked in a bed
But not getting lucky or laid
I paid too much for these sheets
For the colors to fade
Before the end of my life
And they treated me nice…
For a time

No rise and shine
Back in the day,
I wouldn't be snoring
'Til four in the morning
Stayed awake
With the pouring rain
Trained my brain
To like the way
Those sheets felt

Complacency remained
Until I sought shelter elsewhere

Now I rise and shine
At five a.m.
No friction on that end
Unless I have a guest
But even then
I won't allow them
To fuck with my routine
This princess needs
Her beauty sleep
And boundaries are
My new favorite thing
Go on, test me

I am a fierce advocate
For my own happiness
Limitless potential
While caring for my mental state
Nowadays I feel quite fine
About lying in
The new bed I've made

Unicorn

A sober millennial
Now a source that is credible
Eating feelings like they're edible
But they're not

An empath in waiting
I am openly dating
Excel in communicating
I'll tell you that's the spot

Satisfied with single
Waking from a dreamful sleep
Because the real world
Is something I forgot

Time lapses backwards
Rhymes catching faster
Walk, trot, canter
No, I cannot stop

I was made to walk
With glitter on my shoulders
Fuck a chip
That's the shit I'm fucking over

Blood that shimmers
Coursing through my veins
Unbridled passion
I can't control the pace
Riding with no saddle
A higher power holds the reigns

Stabilize my shine
Harness all my energy then fly
Maybe you've caught on

To all the equine verses
I can lead you to water
But you have to take the first sip

Just trust me when I repeat
What I'm about to say
My therapist told me this
So it's a fact for which I paid
I'm no average horse
I'm a fucking unicorn

Hole in the Soul

Phase 1
Fall into the hole in my soul
It's gaping and sore
I can't see anything
Fingernails bleeding
As I claw my way out
Reaching for the sun

Phase 2
One foot falls back in
I pray I resist temptation
And I re-stabilize my alignment
Keep on moving

Phase 3
I stroll down the same path
Notice the pit in the ground
And I laugh in the face of danger
Ha ha ha ha!
Successfully avoiding stagnation

Phase 4
Fully endorsed by my higher self
I forge a new path
One with solid earth
Leaving holes in the past
I know I am whole at last

My Old Way of Thinking

Learning to let go
I used to be trapped in thoughts
Of what I would want
And what should be
Coming to me
That way of thinking
Kept me in a state
Of fear and anxiety

Fear of losing
Something I already possessed
Or failure to get
Something I demanded

Living upon a basis
Of unsatisfied demands
Put me in a state of frustration
And continual disturbance
There was no peace to be had

Then I realized there was nothing I needed
So now I'm no longer taking
I'm more apt to giving and receiving

Satisfied with the strength I found in surrendering
Today I have gratitude
And a sense of spiritual security

Coffee Cancellation

Let's meet for coffee at five
I'll look forward to talking more about your life and mine

She's running late...
I text her, "I'm sitting in the window seat"
Then she says what I wished she wouldn't
"I'm sorry, I won't make it"
Followed by, "My boyfriend's grandma is in the hospital"
Damn, that's inconvenient
What are the chances though?

I'll give you the benefit of the doubt and send you all well wishes
Then I saw you this morning and I know what I witnessed
High and floating to other ethers
We both know the truth
You can just say that you relapsed

I'm not here to judge you
I'm here if you want help
I won't allow abuse
Of my most precious commodity
If there's other things on your plate
I don't care where you'd rather be
I would just appreciate
A heads up in the future
But I shouldn't have expected anything

Now that I know you're still using,
I can take a step back and see the full picture
Thank you for showing me a different point of view
For reminding me that a relapse is something
I never want to do

Because lying was exhausting
Denial was what cost me

Lack of trust in myself
We are all unwell
In our own way
I'm just grateful I've recovered
From that seemingly hopeless mental state

Who I Used to Be

Delicious distractions
Fictitious laughter
Padding the background
Of addictive behavior
Associated with irresponsible plays
Patterned in waves

Let go of the role
Go against what I'm told
University turned me against me
Should've attended a seminary
Buried my personality
With dead leaves
Jumped on the pile
Then set fire
And watched ashes burn
Embers fueled smokescreens
It took time
Things
I
Must
Earn
To come out of the haze
College crazed days
Let my mind go to waste

But wasted not
Cause what I got
Was a new reality
Once I stopped
Obsessive thoughts
Gained back my sanity
Now grateful
I'm able
To communicate

How I relate
To the person
I used to be

Two Wolves

All the shades of me
Pray for them
Creed of courage
In written verses
Words worthy of reciting
Saved by the almighty
Pendulum perfect
Hammer on head no longer working
Draw back the curtains

Let light unearth my soul
Bring together parts of my whole
Shadows shone
Resentment leave me alone
Compassion come here
And don't ever let me go

Merging two lives
Like a stage with two shows
Like two wolves in the forest
One light and one dark

Molding into one person
All the shades of me
Simply dependent
On whichever one
I choose to feed

No Longer a Liar

Trust me when I say,
I'm a great liar
Honestly, you can believe me
Because I'm honest now
My life demands honesty

A manner of living
In which I pray some good
Will come from my suffering
From my mistakes, failures,
Losses and difficulties

After the distress has
Left me and gone
The good I do each day
In its place will live on

I can offer hope to those
Unfortunate souls
Who come face to face
With twin-like troubles

I can turn it into good
My painful experiences
Can now be used
For the betterment of all
So while I may be a great liar
It doesn't have to be that way anymore

Old Acquaintances and New Conceptions

I've seen you before
Not in this way
But in some other story of God
You must've swam out too far
Then tapered off
Like me
You didn't know when to stop
Or what to believe in
Swallowed by the sheer idea of even trying to live life
Without a substance to smother the structure of a mind
But it's without it that I grew to know a divine power,
One that didn't reach out
But was always there

Remember?
We sat in chairs and learned about Jesus
At the time it was all I believed in
But it wasn't enough
My God burst out of the box
I was taught to trap it in,
Crazy the way I always thought I was a victim like "Him,"
Being dragged to Sunday Mass
Sit, stand, sit, stand

My inner compass
Was composed of
Another's beliefs
And now I keep an open mind

I see God in the trees,
In how my body breathes,
In basement rooms,
In secret communities
And I don't hurt like I used to

Now I'm just a human experiencing divinity,
Congeniality comes first in my holy trinity,
In this place, I'm no longer disturbed
So one day I hope to welcome you
To my kind of church

Rocky Bottoms

Stand up tall
On that rocky bottom
They'll try to push you down
But you can stop them
Those feelings of inadequacy
Don't listen to them
Listen to me

You are valued
You are worthy
Stay grounded
You are deserving
Of love

Rocks crumble beneath you
But keep those feet steady
Grab my hand if you need to
We'll stand cliffside and ready

As the tide rises
It will try
To compromise
Your shoreline
Do not avert your eyes
See it for what it is -
LIES

Keep those feet planted
Come hell or high water
Stand up tall
On that rocky bottom

A Moment of Silence

A moment of silence for the lost souls who never found home in spite of riotous despair.

A moment of silence for the sick and suffering who convinced themselves that no community could carry the weights they chose to bear.

They didn't comprehend that a problem becomes halved once it's shared.

A moment of silence for those who never spoke about the toll of discontentment, eventually forming a full-fledged resentment against life itself.

What a hell to live in.

A moment of silence for all those who never outstretched their hands to try and reach for heaven when all the while it was something consciously created.

You might've attained it too. If only you had kept looking.

A moment of silence for those who saw no way of escape from a pain so daunting.

For those fettered by seemingly unbreakable chains.

A moment of silence for the souls who wandered this earth like hungry ghosts waiting to welcome death.

A moment of silence for the ones who are no longer with us and for the ones who pleaded for the end.

Spark of Hope

We move upwards
Progressing from a bottom
For so long unheard
Saw steps but wouldn't follow

An illness of free will
Feelings unfelt will remain unhealed
Growing distant from self
Freedom elusive and distilled
I want out but can't find
A lit path out of hell

Darkness fell and continues to fall
In order to escape
I begin to crawl
Climbing rocky walls
And needing a foothold
I realize I want direction
I want to be told
How to find the light

Tired of trying
And hoping I might
Change on my own
I simply want a map
That will show me
How to get home

On my journey of the soul
I'd never felt so alone
I searched for self-love
So I wouldn't need anyone

But it was in a community setting
That my soul could express

The love I had cultivated
Never regretting
The people who saved me
Showed me the light in the dark
So I could find my way out
By following their spark
Of hope

Primary Purpose

We have a primary purpose
One proven solution
We must pass on
The message -

Attraction
Over
Promotion

We cannot get distracted
From our goal -
To stay sober
To infect everyone
With a vaccine of hope
Like a prospector
Who strikes gold
Then insists on giving it all away

Recovery depends on unity
United we stand
Divided we may sway
Back and forth
Inching ever closer to death's door

But we implore you to listen
To make it *your* mission
To engage in remission
Let go, gain acceptance
Clean house, then offer assistance

We must give this to others
We must be of service
This is our primary purpose

Carry Your Message

With courage I earned
With wisdom I learned
And now it's my turn
To shed light on some issues

I trust that you too
Have been through some shit
The kind of stuff that you never forget
It sits with you and breeds regret
If you let it

So...don't

Accept that it happened
I look back on it with passion
Because from pain comes passion

Stop asking why it had to be this way
Why you deserved that high cost you paid
You didn't
You deserve the best
If you learned the lessons
It won't happen again
And that's what I've come to understand

We're here for something greater
To escalate to a higher faith
If my mother taught me anything
It's that it's never too late

So don't let your age
Or ink blots on your page
Stop you
Pull through
Cause you need to

This world needs you
It needs us both
And I believe that this is the truth
We have to do it
We just have to

Made in the USA
Middletown, DE
26 February 2022